Learn Phonic Spelling

Colour each picture as you finish each page.

Written by Jillian Harker and Geraldine Taylor
Illustrated by Steve Smallman

Ladybird

Begin to spell

Write the letter that spells the first sound in these words.

b	c	b
m	b	m
s	t	r
t	r	t

Write the two letters that spell the first sound in these words.

fl   b_   br

Fl   sh   pl

Try your skills

Circle the letter or letters that spell the first sound in these words.

flag   black   pen

frog   cup   cheese

wig   plug   sun

Parent point: Hearing and writing the sounds that begin words is the first step to building spelling skills. 'I spy' is a useful family game to encourage this skill.

Make a new word

Change the first letter and write the word that rhymes.

I am a wet pet.

cat — bat, hat, mse

fan — man, pan, van

bag — rag, tag, wag

hen — men, ten, pen

net

~~set~~ wet jet

big dig pig weg

Try your skills

Write the rhyming words.

bcat hat rhymes with mat

sot tot rhymes with mor

rmp rhymes with lip

Parent point: Making new words by changing the first letter helps improve awareness of letter patterns. Play rhyming games with your children.

Find the missing sound

I'm a bug in a bag.

Write the missing letter to make the correct word.

a or e?

b_g   b_g   p_n   p_n   m_n   m_n

a or i?

f_t   f_t   p_t   p_t   t_p   t_p

a or u?

r_g   r_g   b_g   b_g   t_g   t_g

a or o ?

m_p   m_p   s_ck   s_ck   bl_ck   bl_ck

e or u ?

b_d   b_d   n_t   n_t   d_ck   d_ck

Try your skills

Write the correct word.

_____   _____

_____   _____   _____   _____

Parent point: Recognising vowel sounds in the middle of words is a keystone of spelling.

Rhyme and spell

I jog on a log.

Write the same ending to make a new rhyming word.

lip   p＿＿   r＿＿   t＿＿

dog   f＿＿   l＿＿   j＿＿

hop   m＿＿   p＿＿   t＿＿

jug   m＿＿   t＿＿   r＿＿

can

p__

f__

v__

bin

f__

t__

p__

Try your skills

Complete the word under the picture and write words that rhyme with it.

s__ rhymes with _____ _____ _____

p__ rhymes with _____ _____ _____

Parent point: Make a set of cards to help your child understand that rhyming words are often written with the same letter pattern. Build words by joining different letters of the alphabet to the same ending, eg, **b**ad, **p**ad, **m**ad.

Finish the words

Complete the word using an **ee** pattern.

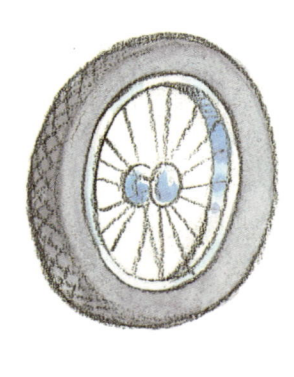

"I s**ee** the m**oo**n."

b**__**

j**__**p

p**__**l

tr**__**

wh**__**l

thr**__**

h**__**l

w**__**p

sl**__**p

Finish the word using an **oo** pattern.

m__n n__n sp__n

b__t r__t sh__t

c__l t__l st__l

Try your skills

Use **ee** or **oo** to make the correct word.

p__l p__l

sh__t sh__t

g__se g__se

Parent point: Help your child to listen to the sounds in the middle of words and to notice how the sound is written. (See page 24 for the **ea** spelling of the sound **e**.)

Building words

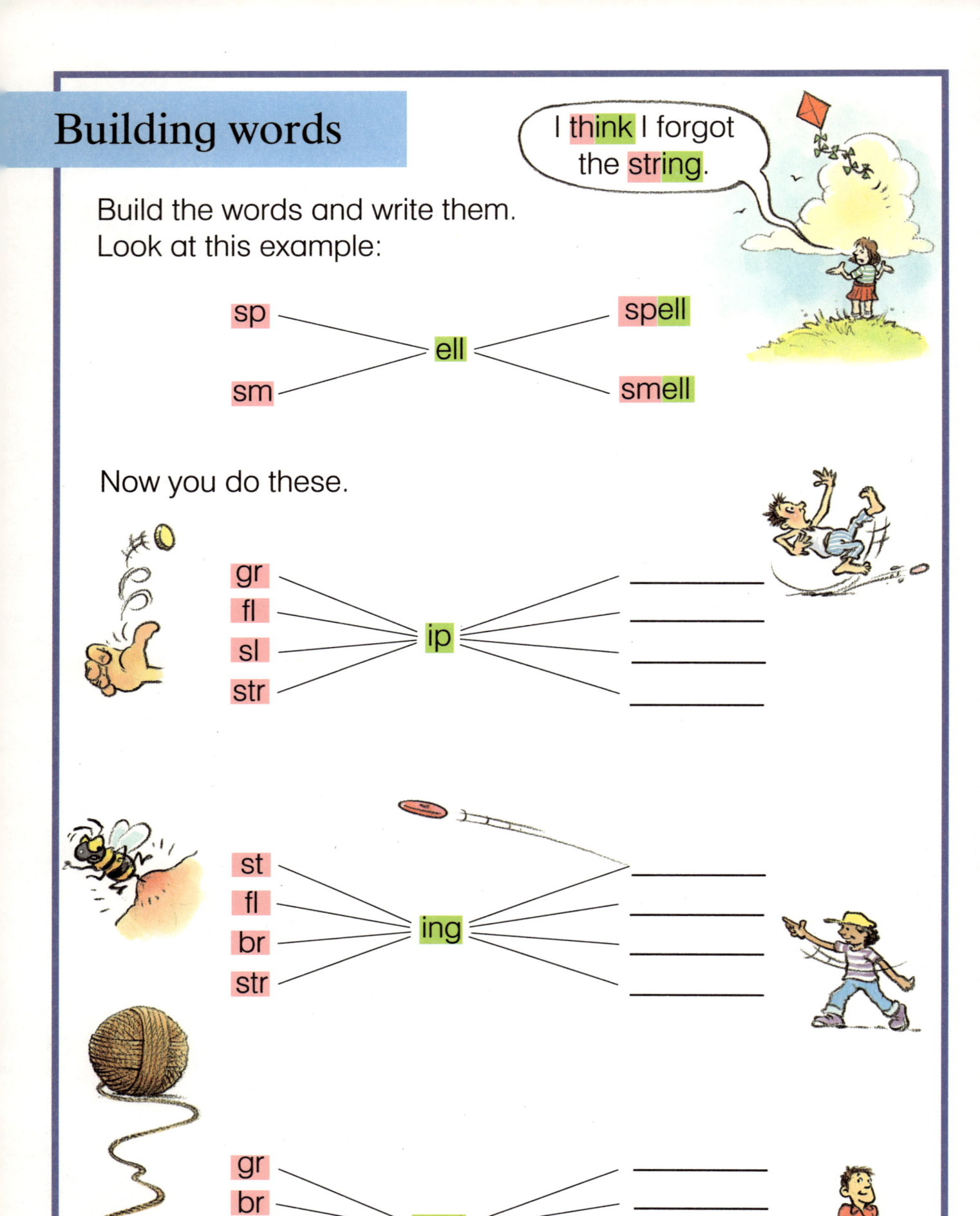

"I think I forgot the string."

Build the words and write them.
Look at this example:

sp ─┐   ┌─ spell
    ├─ ell ─┤
sm ─┘   └─ smell

Now you do these.

gr ─┐
fl ─┤
sl ─┼─ ip ─ _____
str ┘   _____
             _____
             _____

st ─┐
fl ─┤
br ─┼─ ing ─ _____
str ┘   _____
              _____
              _____

gr ─┐
br ─┤
st ─┼─ and ─ _____
str ┘   _____
              _____
              _____

12

| dr |
| th |
| bl |
| shr |

ink

_____
_____
_____
_____

| fr |
| gr |
| sp |
| thr |

ill

_____
_____
_____
_____

Try your skills

Draw a line to match the beginnings to the endings and write the words.

| pl |
| sn |
| spl |
| sch |

| ool |
| ash |
| um |
| ip |

_____
_____
_____
_____

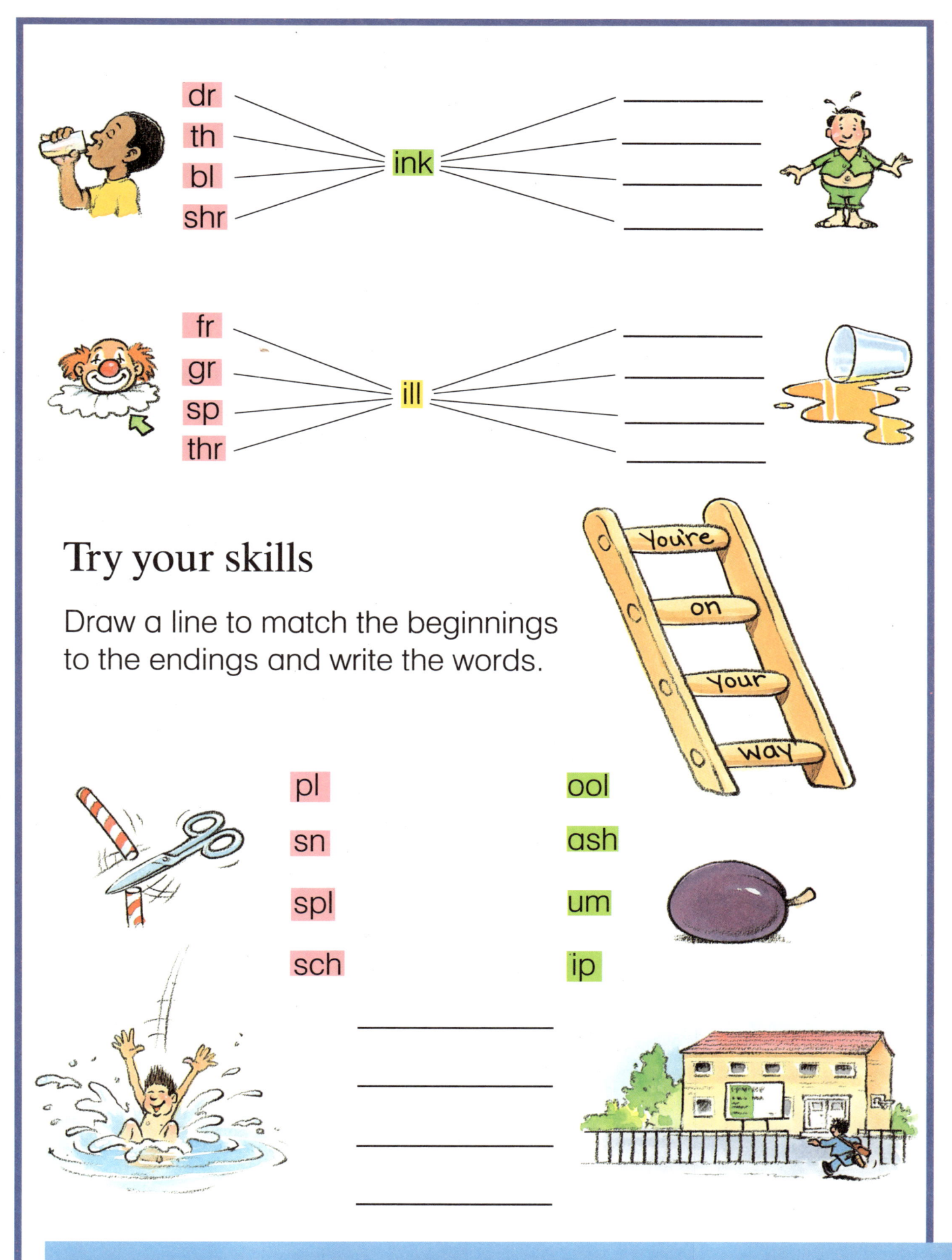

Parent point: Using letter strings to build words marks a development in spelling skills.

Using words

Three geese slip into a cool pool.

These are some of the words you have made.
Use the right ones to complete each sentence.

spill   string   grip   drink   bring   sting   slip

Be careful, the bee may _____.

Don't _____ your _____.

Will you _____ me some _____?

He has lost his _____ and his hands will _____.

14

Here are some more words you have made.
Use them to describe the pictures.

p**oo**l   b**ee**s   j**ee**p   tr**ee**   thr**ee**   c**oo**l   wh**ee**ls

_____ _____ around a _____

_____ four _____ on a _____

a frog in a _____ _____

Try your skills

Can you remember how to spell these words?

_ _ _ _   _ _ _ _   _ _ _ _ _

_ _ _ _ _   _ _ _ _ _ _   _ _ _ _ _ _

Parent point: It is important for children to be able to use spelling skills when they write real sentences. Encourage as much writing as you can.

Silent e

I like a nice ice-cream.

Say the words and listen to the sounds.
Add the silent **e** to change the word.

tap into **tape**

Now you do these.

cap into _____

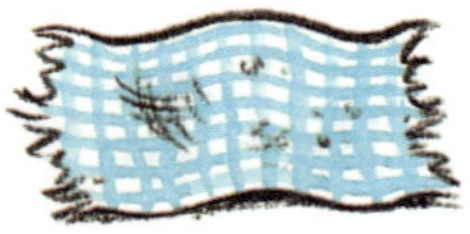

rag into _____

pin into _____

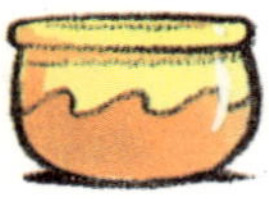

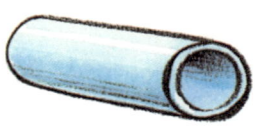

tub into _____

stag into _____

Link

Word Ladders

A game for 1–4 players.
You will need:
a dice
a counter or button each.
pencils and paper

1. Place the counter(s) on the start.
2. Each player in turn rolls the dice and follows the arrows (via any blue circle) around the track. Write down the first word on which you land
3. Change one letter of your word to make a new word. Repeat this to make as long a list as you can. Do not repeat the word with which you started. Score 1 point for each new word.
   Example:
   fan
   can
   man
   map
   Score: 4 points
4. Repeat 2 and 3 as you move around and back to the start.
5. Add up your score. The winner is the player with the most points.

Try several tracks and see how you improve.
HINT: Build up a ladder of rhyming words before changing the second or third letter.

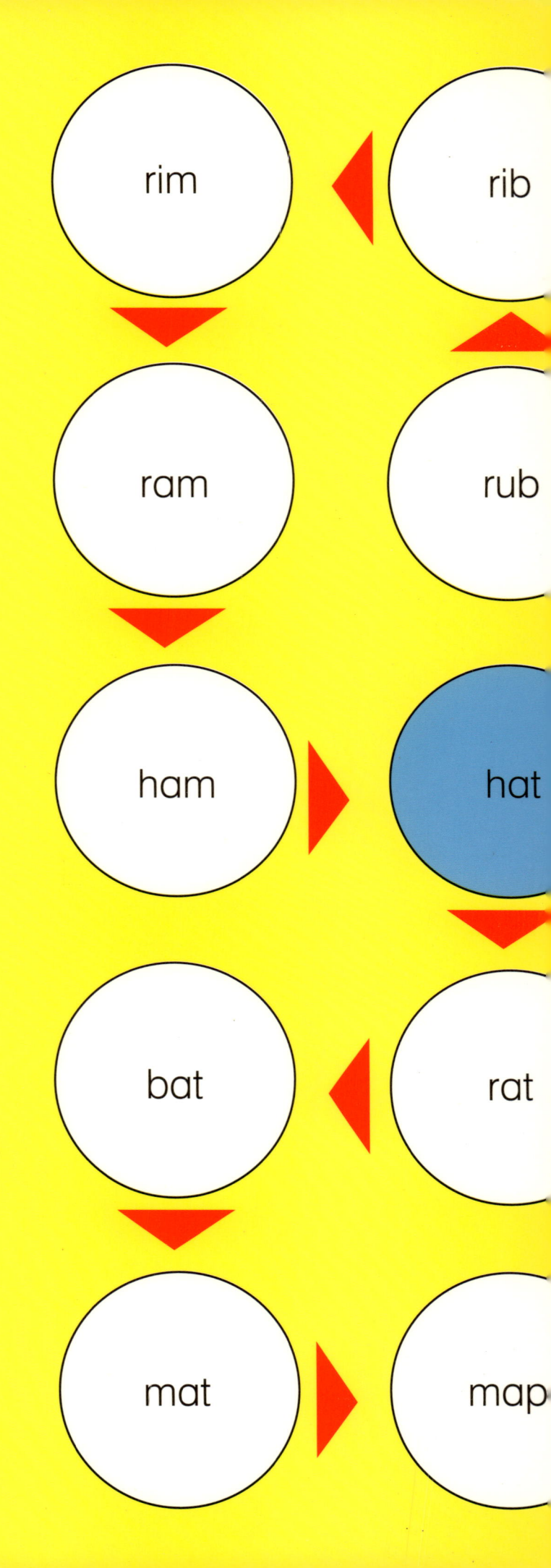

rim — rib
ram — rub
ham — hat
bat — rat
mat — map

bun ◀ bin ◀ fin

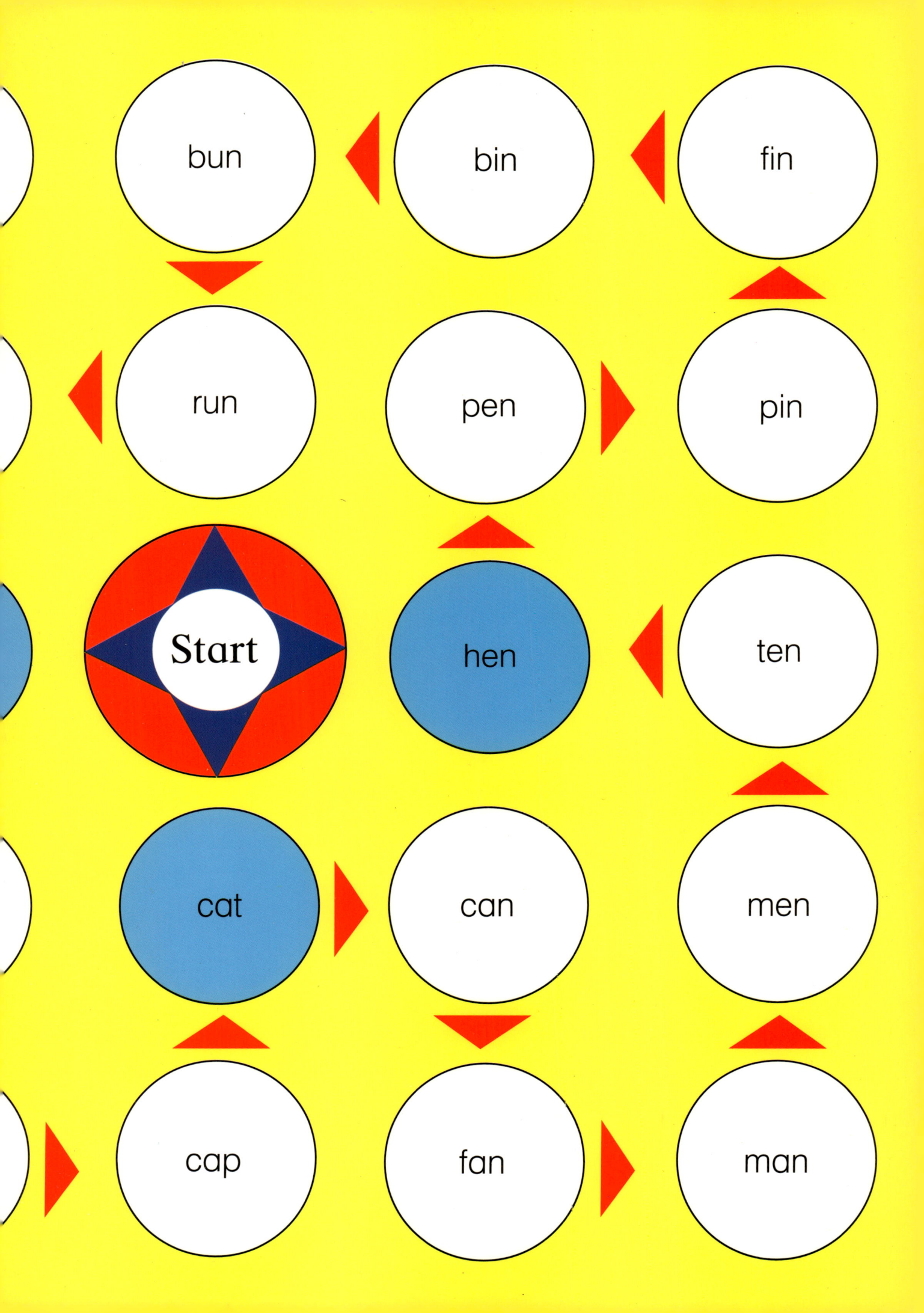

run pen ▶ pin

Start hen ◀ ten

cat ▶ can men

cap fan ▶ man

Links: picture-word game

This is a game for one player.

1. Write the letters of the alphabet on pieces of card (you could use plastic magnetic letters).
2. Lay out the alphabet cards in order on the table.
3. Start on any blue circle and mark your place with a counter or a button.
4. Look at the picture and choose the three correct letter cards to spell out the word.
5. Follow the arrow and change one letter to make the new word. (Make sure you put the other letter back into the alphabet in the right place.)
6. Work round the track changing one letter for each new word.

Time yourself. How long does it take you to get back to the beginning? Start on a different blue circle. Can you get right round faster this time?

Check your routes on the reverse of this card.

kit into _____

pan into _____

win into _____

Try your skills

Write the words under the pictures.
Circle the words that have the silent **e**.

_____ _____

_____ _____

_____ _____

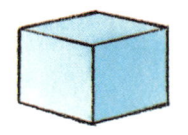

Parent point: Understanding the change made to the sound of a word by adding the silent **e** is a vital development in spelling.

More silent e

I'm going to t**ake** a sl**ice** of c**ake**.

Read these silent **e** words out loud.
Circle the matching letter patterns.

f(ace)

take

l(ace)

late

wake

r(ace)

mine

hate

lake

hope

pine

date

shake

nice

cope

fine

grate

ice

mope

shine

price

slope

spice

Use the patterns you have seen to spell these words.

_____   _____   _____

_____   _____   _____

_____   _____   _____

Try your skills

Write two more words to rhyme with these.

h**ose**   s**a**m**e**   w**i**d**e**

_____   _____   _____

_____   _____   _____

Climbing high

Parent point: Take every opportunity to read, find and talk about words with a silent e.

Middle sounds

"I leave a trail on the beach."

Complete these words using an **ea** pattern.

r__d   b__d   l__d   b__n

r__l   m__l   l__f   st__l

n__t   m__t   h__t   b__ch

Now use an **ai** pattern.

r__n   tr__n   st__n   p__nt

s__l   t__l   n__l   spr__n

r__l   p__r   h__r   ch__r

Now read all the words on this page. Circle the word in each line that does not rhyme with the other three.

Can you spell these words?

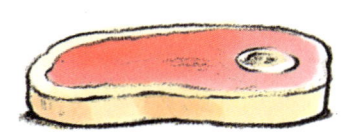

_____   _____   _____

_____   _____   _____

_____   _____   _____

Try your skills

Fill in the missing words to complete the sentences.

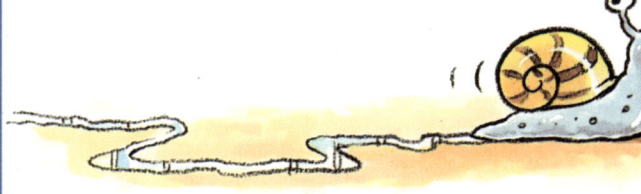

A _____ leaves a _____ .

There's a _____ on the _____ .

My friend has _____ _____ .

Parent point: It is important that children understand that a single sound may be written with more than one letter.

21

Doing words (verbs)

I'm splashing and swimming.

Look at the word **splash** and see what happens to it in the sentence.

The girl is splashing in the puddle.

Use these words in the same way.

jump   The dog is _____ over the log.

paint   The painter is _____ the door.

float   The feather is _____ on the pond.

roar   The lion is _____ loudly.

smell   The woman is _____ the flowers.

Now look very carefully at the word **hop** and see what happens to it in the sentence.

The frog is hop**ping**.

Use these words in the same way.

dig The girl is _____ the garden.

pop The boy is _____ the balloon.

hug The baby is _____ the teddy bear.

cut The baker is _____ the cake.

flap The flag is _____ in the wind.

Try your skills

Put each word into your own sentence.

hit**ting** _____

brush**ing** _____

pick**ing** _____

slip**ping** _____

Parent point: Help your child to notice which verbs contain double letters when **ing** is added: hop, hopping, and which do not: jump, jumping. Use the examples on this page to help you.

Same sound – different patterns

I'm **ea**ting a sw**ee**t p**ea**ch.

Use the **ea** pattern to complete these words.

l__k   dr__m   p__ch

l__p   b__k

l__ves   __gle   st__m

s__side   s__son

Read the words and listen to the sound pattern.

Now complete these words using the **ee** pattern.

f__t   sw__t   kn__l

scr__n   asl__p   str__t

Read the words and listen to the sound pattern.

Try your skills

Write the word under the picture. Remember to use the correct pattern – **ee** or **ea**.

The _____ are falling from the _____ .

Would you like a _____ to _____ ?

The _____ has sharp claws on his _____ .

Parent point: Help your child to notice that the same sound can be written with a different letter pattern in different words.

Different patterns – same sound

Owls fly without a sound.

Use the **ou** pattern to complete these words.

h__se

cl__d

sh__t

sc__t

gr__nd

ar__nd

b__nce

m__ntain

m__se

c__nt

sp__t

bl__se

s__nd

th__sand

p__nce

f__ntain

Read the words and listen to the sound pattern.

Read these words with the **ow** pattern.

owl	town	clowns	frown
tower	shower	flower	towel
trowel	eyebrows		

Use the words to complete the sentences.

The _____ is on the _____ .

I need a _____ when I _____ .

The gardener planted the _____ with a _____ .

He pulls his _____ down in a _____ .

The _____ are coming to _____ .

Try your skills

Write the word under the picture.
Remember to use the correct pattern – **ou** or **ow**.

_____   _____   _____

_____   _____   _____

Parent point: Help your child to notice that the same sound can be written with a different letter pattern in different words.

Use your spelling skills

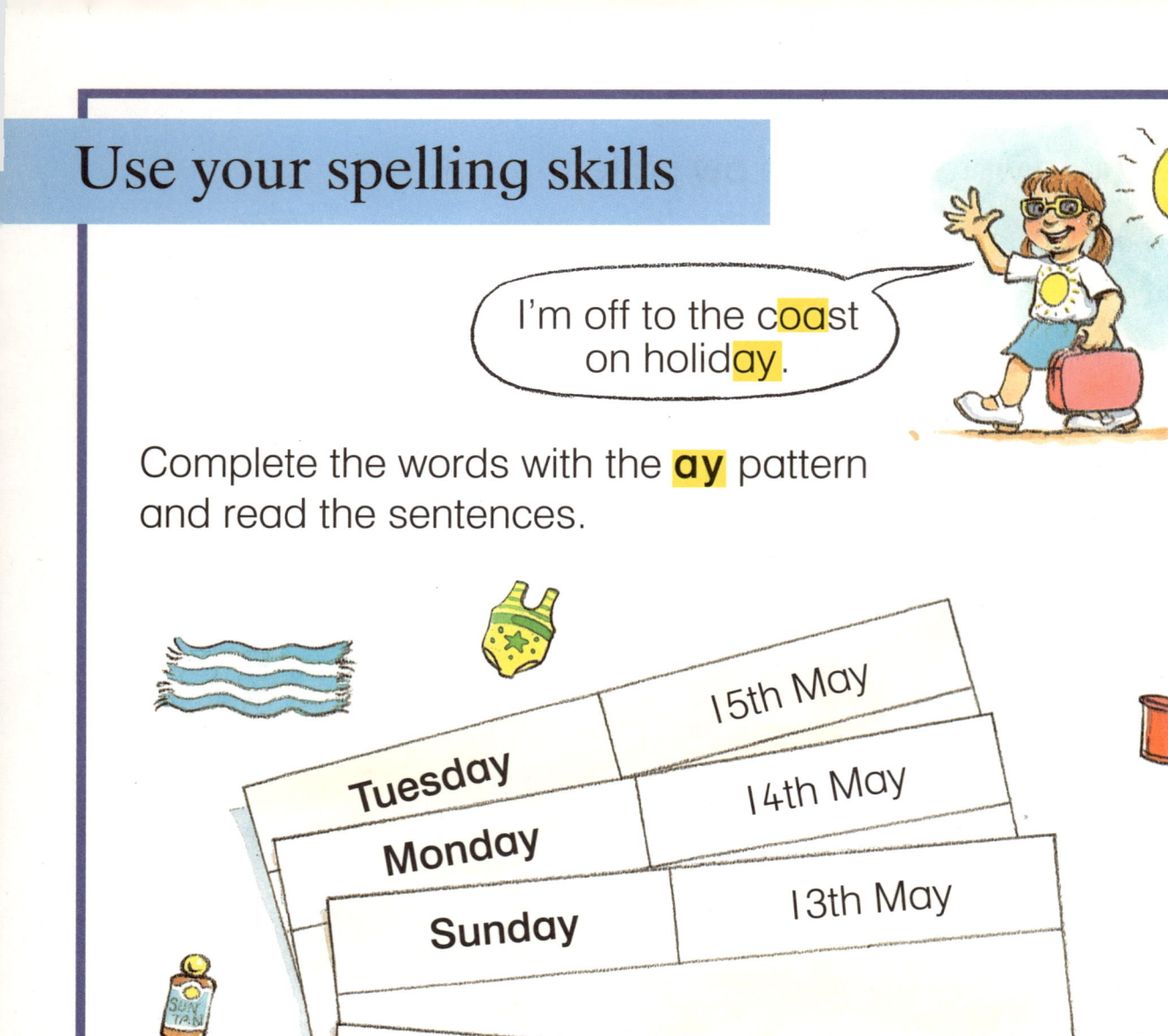

I'm off to the c**oa**st on holid**ay**.

Complete the words with the **ay** pattern and read the sentences.

	15th May
Tuesday	14th May
Monday	13th May
Sunday	
Saturday	12th May

Tod___ is Saturd___, 12th M___ and we are going on holid___.

It is a long w___ so we are going on the railw___. On the train we m___ pl___ with our cr___ons.

28

Complete the words using the **oa** pattern and read the postcard.

Dear Granny,

We went on a c**oa**ch trip yesterday. I forgot my c**oa**t and it rained so I got s**oa**ked. We also went out in a b**oa**t along the c**oa**st. When we came back we had hot coc**oa** and t**oa**st.

Love Joan

Mrs B St**oa**ts
23 **Oa**klands R**oa**d
Oakhampton
OA1 2AY

Try your skills

Congratulations!

Write the words that rhyme with:

fl**oa**t _____   r**oa**d _____

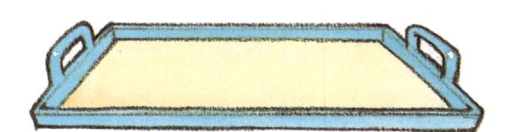

m**ay** _____   s**ay** _____

Parent point: Children need to see that the reason for good spelling is clear communication.

Try your skills

You've reached the top.

Look at the pictures one by one and write each word in the correct mountain.

oo ee
ice ake ea
ai ow
ou ing oa

Parent point: All spelling skills need considerable practice. Help your child to notice and practise writing words that contain the same pattern.

Skills checklist

pages

2 Can write letter for first sound in words: **bag** ☐

3 Understands letter blends at beginning of words: **flag** ☐

4 Sees link between rhyme and letter patterns: **cat, hat** ☐

5 Understands link between rhyme and letter patterns: **rip, lip** ☐

6 Can write middle vowel sound correctly: **tap** ☐

7 Beginning to spell simple words: **hit** ☐

8 Understands link between rhyming words: **mop, hop** ☐

9 Can spell simple rhyming words: **sun, run** ☐

10 Understands **ee** spelling: **jeep** ☐

11 Can distinguish between **ee** and **oo** sound: **peel, pool** ☐

12 Can build words using beginning letter blends **sp + ell** ☐

13 Can build words using beginning letter blends **pl + um** ☐

14 Can use simple spellings in context ☐

15 Remembers spelling patterns ☐

16 Beginning to use **silent e** ☐

pages

17 Understands effect of **silent e** ☐

18 Can distinguish final letter patterns with **silent e** ☐

19 Can use **silent e** letter patterns ☐

20 Can use vowel combinations ☐

21 Can use vowel combinations in spellings ☐

22 Can use final **ing** pattern ☐

23 Understands use of double consonant before final **ing** pattern: **hop, hopping** ☐

24 Can use **ea** pattern: **peach** ☐

25 Can distinguish between **ee** and **ea** pattern. Spells words like **feet, dream** ☐

26 Can use **ou** pattern ☐

27 Can distinguish between **ou** and **ow** pattern. Spells words like **cloud, tower** ☐

28 Can use **ay** pattern ☐

29 Understands use of **oa** and **ay** patterns ☐

30 Remembers spelling patterns practised ☐

31 Can see linking patterns in spellings practised ☐